Make in a Day

POMPOM CRAFTS

Victoria Hudgins

Photography by
Erin Holland

Dover Publications, Inc.
Mineola, New York

Bibliographical Note

Make in a Day: Pompom Crafts is a new work,
first published by Dover Publications, Inc., in 2016.

International Standard Book Number

ISBN-13: 978-0-486-81084-3
ISBN-10: 0-486-81084-4

Manufactured in the United States
81084401   2016
www.doverpublications.com

CONTENTS

Crafting has always been a passion of mine; from the earliest days I can remember I was designing and creating. Being able to use this love of creation to bless my family and friends through parties, gatherings, and gifts is a big reason I create books and blog daily at **asubtlerevelry.com.**

Revelry. Everywhere. Every day. I believe in living a lifestyle of celebration. Taking up our stashes of confetti, just to make every day feel special. Baking cakes just because they taste good, and because that cake stand is too pretty to be sitting in the cabinet! Crafting to make every part of life prettier. Enjoying every moment. Because Revelry is waiting for us everywhere— you only have to create it.

With a background in interior design and event planning, I love combining my skills and passions to create books, the blog, and my social media spaces. With thousands of followers worldwide, I've been styling, creating, and sharing a festive lifestyle for over seven years.

Crafting with pompoms can be such great fun! One of the earliest crafts I remember doing was creating a fun wedding toss out of pompoms. Pompoms have now become quite the crafting craze, with the decorative yarn balls being stocked in almost every store and crafted in hundreds of different ways. They can be used to gussy up almost anything imaginable to instantly add a dash of pizzazz to home décor items. Included here are a number of fun craft ideas and creative ways to make and use pompoms at home. Let's jump in!

Victoria Hudgins

Pompom Baskets

Creating a custom look for an everyday wicker basket makes it much more special. Whether you use these sweet baskets for party favors, Easter gifts, or bathroom storage, or to brighten up your office desk—they are adorable and will instantly perk up the space.

To make the pompom baskets, you will need:

* Medium weight yarn in various colors

* Small baskets

* Scissors

* Fork

* Hot glue gun

* Candy or party favors

1 Start by creating the pompoms. Wrap the yarn about 10–15 times around the fork. Tie a knot through the middle.

2 Take the yarn off the fork and cut the sides to form a pompom. Trim the pompom if necessary.

3 Using a hot glue gun, attach the pompoms to the front of the basket, along the top edge.

4 Fill the baskets with candy, party favors, or other treats!

Pompom Bunnies

These cute pompom bunnies might be one of my favorite pompom crafts ever! They are adorable and would be super cute to use as party favors, small gifts for friends, or as desktop decorations. They would also be charming to display in a nursery or a child's playroom.

To make the pompom bunnies, you will need:

* Medium weight yarn in various colors
* Large pompom maker
* Small pompom maker
* Large cotton ball for the tail
* Small cotton ball for the nose
* Scissors
* Hot glue gun
* Cardstock paper for the ears
* Tinsel or jewelry wire for the whiskers

1 Start by creating the pompoms for the body and the head in the same color. Use the large pompom maker for the body and the small pompom maker for the head.

Wrap the yarn around the pompom maker until there is a large bulge on one side and you can't see the plastic. Repeat this on the other side.

Cut both sides of the yarn while the pompom is still on the maker. Tie a knot in the middle before releasing the pompom from the maker and trim if necessary.

2 Cut out the ears from the cardstock paper, making a larger ear shape in one color and a smaller ear shape in a contrasting color.

3 Attach the bunny ears to the head using the hot glue gun. Next, attach the whiskers to the back side of the nose. Attach the back side of the nose to the head using the hot glue gun.

4 Use a small piece of yarn to connect the head to the body; it works best to tie the yarn around the ties that were used to create the pompom to allow the bunnies to keep their shape.

5 Make more bunnies in varying colors. Now your bunnies are ready for action!

Pompom Cake Toppers

Topping a party cake doesn't take awesome bakery skills when you have pompoms! Create this fun party scene by hanging pompoms as a backdrop and tossing a few around the cake for good measure. These fun yarn pompom poofs are perhaps the simplest and least expensive projects of all, but they are one of my all-time favorites! Make them in bright colors for an upcoming party or in white as a snowy winter decoration.

To make the pompom cake toppers, you will need:

* Medium weight yarn in various colors

* Scissors

* Fishing line

* Cake doily or parchment paper cut slightly smaller than the top of your cake

* Optional: fresh flower

1 Start by creating the pompoms. Wrap the yarn about 30-40 times around three fingers to create a thick, tight circle.

2 Gently remove the yarn from fingers and tie a knot around the middle.

3 Cut the sides to form a pompom and trim the pompom if necessary.

4 Tie the pompom balls onto the fishing line and hang in a random pattern over the cake table.

5 Place a cake doily or parchment paper on your cake and adorn with a few colorful pompoms. Toss a few pompoms and flowers around the cake stand to create a great party look.

Pompom Office Supplies

Making a desk attractive and appealing helps everyone work more efficiently—don't you agree? Create these fun pompom pencils and bookmarks for an office that will inspire you to get working!

To make the pompom office supplies, you will need:

* Medium weight yarn in various colors

* Fork

* Pencils

* Large-eye sewing needle

* Embroidery thread in contrasting color to yarn

* Large paper clips

* Optional: white craft glue

1 Start by creating the miniature pompoms. Wrap a thick layer of yarn 40 times around the fork. Tie a knot through the middle and take the yarn off the fork. Cut the sides to form a pompom.

To get tight, ball-shaped pompoms, trim the yarn down closer to the center than you normally would. Keep cutting until your pompom looks like a dense ball.

2 Next, make the tassels using embroidery thread. Cut about 50 6"-lengths. Tie a 12" piece of thread around the middle of the threads.

3 Fold in half and tie about ¹/₂" from the top with another piece of thread in a contrasting color to hold in place.

Next, thread the remaining longer piece of embroidery thread through a needle and guide the needle up and through the center of the pompom. Push the pompom down until it meets the tassel. Now the longer piece of thread can be used to attach the tassel to a pencil or paper clip.

4 For the pencils—remove the erasers and glue the tassel into the eraser bed before replacing the eraser.

5 For the bookmarks—tie the tassel thread around large paper clips.

Pompom Straws

Kick your next gathering up a notch with a handful of pompom-clad straws. These straws are great fun and are so simple to make. You'll be thrilled to have this festive party detail come together with ease and beauty.

To make the pompom straws, you will need:

* Lightweight yarn in various colors
* Small pompom maker
* Plastic or paper decorative party straws

1 Start by making the pompoms. Wrap the yarn around one side of the pompom maker until there is a large bulge and you can't see the plastic. Repeat this on the other side.

For most pompom projects I like using thicker yarn, but these straws really look cute with thin yarn as well—just make sure it is wrapped well before removing.

Cut both sides of the yarn while the pompom is still on the maker and trim if necessary. Tie a knot around the middle firmly, leaving enough ease to push the straw through later. Release the pompom from the maker.

2 Take the straw and gently thread it up and through the center tie of the pompom.

3 Push the pompom into place so it allows your guests to drink easily from the straw without getting yarn in their mouth.

4 Keep making pompoms in various colors. You can wrap more or less yarn around the pompom maker to vary the thickness of the pompoms.

5 Display your pompom straws in festive paper cups for guests to enjoy!

Pompom Gift Wrap

Top all of your presents in a unique and customized style using yarn pompoms—it's prettier than wrapping with plain paper.

To make the pompom gift wrap, you will need:

* Bulky weight yarn in various colors

* Large pompom maker

* Scissors

* Decorative ribbons (16") in contrasting color to yarn

* Gift boxes

1 Start by making the pompoms in the large pompom maker.

Wrap the yarn of your choice around one side of the pompom maker until there is a large bulge and you can't see the plastic. Repeat this on the other side.

Cut both sides of the yarn while the pompom is still on the maker and trim if necessary. Tie a knot in the middle before releasing the pompom from the maker.

Tip: When you tie the pompom, be sure to leave the ends long so that you can tie them in step 2.

2 After making the large pompom, take the two long strands of yarn and tie them around the center of a ribbon.

3 You can include a gift tag on the boxes as well—draw the yarn through the tag's hole and then onto the ribbon.

4 Using a small piece of tape, attach the ribbon and pompom to the top of the gift box. Use one large pompom on a small box for a festive graphic punch, or create the look on a large box by tying 2 to 4 pompoms along the length of one ribbon before attaching it to the box.

5 Gift-giving will feel even more special when you wrap your gift in this handmade decorative box.

Pompom Pendant

Looking for a way to decorate a new home? Look no further than this fun and furry pompom light fixture. The entire piece brings a touch of flair to your space, and the colors of the yarn can be altered to make the piece fit any space—from a kid's room (think pretty pastels or bright hues) to a more formal reading corner (grays). This pompom pendant is so much fun that it is sure to garner smiles every time you flip the light switch.

To make the pompom pendant, you will need:

* 1 white paper lantern light fixture with socket kit

* Scissors

* Hot glue gun

* Medium weight yarn in various colors for about 60 small pompoms

* Optional: needle and thread

1 Make the pompom pendant by starting with a white lantern lamp base and a few of your favorite colors of yarn.

You'll need to make about 60 simple yarn pompoms. This part is a little time-consuming, but well worth the effort!

2 To make the pompoms, wrap the yarn about 30–40 times around three fingers.

3 Gently pull the yarn off your fingers and tie a knot around the middle.

4 Cut the sides to form a pompom and trim if necessary.

5 Once the pompoms are made, attach them to the light. You could easily do this using hot glue, although for a longer-lasting pendant you can take a needle and thread and guide the thread through the center of each pompom and attach it to the light with a simple stitch

Hang the light fixture with a plug-in cord from an eyehook in the ceiling, or hardwire it into a light socket and enjoy!

Pompom Confetti Magnets

Brighten up the fridge and find a fun way to hold up those important papers with this pompom confetti magnet. It's one of those little details I love adding for a simple but effective way to create a fun home.

To make the pompom confetti magnets, you will need:

* Thick multi-color twine or cotton yarn

* Medium pompom maker

* Thick rectangular magnets

* Scissors

* Craft glue

1 Start by creating the pompoms with the multi-color twine. Using this type of twine is an easy way to create pompoms with a fun texture and vibrant look.

2 Wrap the twine around one side of the pompom maker until there is a large bulge and you can't see the plastic. Repeat this on the other side.

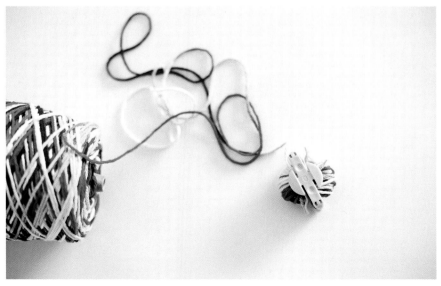

3 Cut both sides of the twine while the pompom is still on the maker. Tie a knot in the middle before releasing the pompom from the maker and trim if necessary.

Fluff one half of the pompom and make the back side as flat as possible. The back side is where the magnet will be attached.

4 Glue the back side of the pompom onto the magnet. It is important for this project that you use sturdy, thick magnets—not the tiny circular types—as the magnet will be used to hold both the pompom and your papers or photos.

5 Fluff out the top portion of the pompom and trim the uneven ends if needed before placing it on the fridge.

2 Tie a knot through the middle and take the yarn off the fork.

3 Cut the sides to form a pompom and trim if necessary.

Make a batch of about 8–14 pompoms in various colors and sizes, depending on the size of your headband. Wrap 20–30 times around the fork to create smaller pompoms.

4 Tie the pompoms in random formation onto a thick headband. As the pompoms are added to the headband, some will naturally move forward, creating a full, layered look.

5 Once all the pompom bunches are attached to the headband, cut a small section of felt in a similar color as the headband. Glue the felt along the inside of the headband to hide all the pompom ties.

Pompoms for Dish Towels

Brighten up the kitchen without the hassle of remodeling by adding spunky details such as these pompoms for dish towels. They are a fun way to add vibrant touches, and they look great hanging from the stove or when serving afternoon coffee to your guests.

To make the pompoms for dish towels, you will need:

* Dish towels

* Yarn in various weights and colors

* Small pompom maker

* Scissors

* A length of miniature pompom trimming in the same width as your towel

* Needle and thread

1 Start by making the pompoms. Wrap the yarn around one side of the pompom maker until there is a large bulge and you can't see the plastic. Repeat this on the other side.

2 Cut both sides of the yarn while the pompom is still on the maker. Tie a knot in the middle before releasing the pompom from the maker and trim if necessary.

3 Make several pompoms in various weights and colors. Hand-sew the miniature pompom trim along the bottom edges of the dish towel to add extra pompom detail if desired. Do this before attaching the handmade pompoms.

4 Attach the handmade pompoms with thread and needle to the bottom of each dish towel. It actually works best to attach these twice—first threading through the front part of the dish towel and the center of the pompom, and then again through the center of the pompom but a little to the right or left of the first stitch. This keeps the pompoms securely in place when the dish towel is used for serving and hanging.

5 Use the decorated dish towels to adorn a serving tray, adding elegance and color.

Pompom Wall Flags

Whether you are looking for something fun to decorate the walls for a temporary celebration or for something more permanent—these paper and pompom wall flags are a great way to fill a large space fast. They are bright and can be made to say anything from "Feast" for a family party to a child's name displayed over a bed.

To make the pompom wall flags, you will need:

* Large, colorful poster board in various colors

* Long wooden dowel

* Bulky weight yarn in various colors

* Scissors

* Large pompom maker

* Adhesive boat decal letters (can be purchased at any home improvement store)

* Hot glue gun

* Optional: colored ribbon

1 Start by creating the pompoms. Wrap the yarn around one side of the pompom maker until there is a large bulge and you can't see the plastic. Repeat this on the other side.

Cut both sides of the yarn while the pompom is still on the maker. Tie a knot in the middle before releasing the pompom from the maker and trim if necessary.

2 Next, make the flags—cut the large poster board into flag shapes as shown in the photo. Cut some flags larger than others so you can fit the boat decal letters as shown in step 3.

3 Use the boat decal letters to fill in the words of your choice on the largest of the flags. We used "FEAST" and "JOY."

42

4 Attach each flag to the wooden dowel with hot glue along the back.

5 Use an 18–24" length of the yarn or ribbon to attach the pompom to the wooden dowel by tying off at the top for the perfect festive party detail.

Pompom Flowers

Here's a fun bouquet that won't ever wilt! No green thumbs needed, just a little yarn and paper—my favorite kind of flower. This bouquet is a sweet gift for a beloved mom or teacher. Or make a set of the flowers to keep for yourself—they look great adorning a mantel.

To make the pompom flowers, you will need:

* Bulky weight yarn in various colors

* Large pompom maker

* Colorful tissue paper to match the yarn colors

* Thick wrapped floral wire

* Stapler

* Hot glue gun

1 Start by creating the pompoms. You will need one pompom per flower.

Wrap the yarn around one side of the pompom maker until there is a large bulge and you can't see the plastic. Repeat this on the other side.

Cut both sides of the yarn while the pompom is still on the maker. Tie a knot in the middle before releasing the pompom from the maker and trim if necessary.

2 Create the flower back with tissue paper. The tissue flowers are made by accordion-folding 5 sheets of tissue paper together, making 1½" pleats. Fold the paper in the middle and staple directly in the center of the fold.

3 Unfold, and cut a scallop-shaped edge into both sides of the tissue paper strip. The last step is to carefully begin pulling the tissue layers out from each other until the flower is formed.

4 Cut a length of the thick wrapped floral wire to the desired height of the pompom flower stem. Hot glue the floral wire to the back of each of the tissue flowers.

5 Using hot glue again, top the paper flowers with the pompoms and combine for a bouquet that will last all year long!

Pompoms for Pillows

Nothing beats a pillow with fun details for livening up a bed or sofa. The addition of pompoms to any pillow instantly gives it a custom style and a special look. You could make these pillows from scratch, find great-looking vintage designs, or use store-bought designs that need extra pizzazz.

To make the pompoms for pillows, you will need:

* Decorative pillows

* Medium pompom maker

* Large pompom maker

* Hand-sewing needle and thread

* Bulky weight yarn to coordinate with the pillows and the home décor

* Scissors

1 Start by creating the pompoms. I like the look of four large pompoms for the corners of a pillow, or make a number of medium pompoms to run up the side of a pillow. Wrap the yarn around one side of the pompom maker until there is a large bulge on one side and you can't see the plastic. Repeat this on the other side.

2 Cut both sides of the yarn while the pompom is still on the maker. Tie a knot in the middle before releasing the pompom from the maker and trim if necessary.

3 Attach pompoms to the pillow by tying them through the center with the needle and thread and then stitch into either the sides or corners of the pillow.

4 Be sure to hand-stitch the pompoms a number of times—think of how you would securely sew on a button.

5 Fasten off the thread and fluff out the pompoms and pillows for a gorgeous display!

6 These colorful decorated pillows will spice up any décor!

Pompom Party Garland

No party is as pretty as one that has a pompom garland strung around the room. This garland is so much fun, and it makes a huge statement in a festive space for so little time and money. It is the kind of party decoration that leaves you plenty of time to focus on the really important things—such as cake!

There is nothing quite like novelty yarn. Visit your local craft store for versions of this yarn, and look for fun colors or textures that will really set the party garland apart. For such a simple project, details like the yarn type really matter.

To make the pompom party garland, you will need:

* Colorful bulky weight novelty yarn
* Medium pompom maker
* Scissors

1 Start by creating the pompoms. Wrap the yarn around one side of the pompom maker until there is a large bulge and you can't see the plastic. Repeat this on the other side.

2 Cut both sides of the yarn while the pompom is still on the maker. Tie a knot in the middle before releasing the pompom from the maker and trim if necessary.

3 Make as many pompoms as needed for the length of garland desired. The pompoms here are placed about every 10" on the garland.

4 Once all the pompoms are crafted, tie them onto a long strand of yarn to form the garland.

5 Knot a couple of times and trim ends of ties.

6 String up the garlands in the party room, along with decorative paper honeycombs. Use the garlands to celebrate any occasion!

Pompom Heart Wreath

Create a cozy corner of the house or provide a warm welcome to visitors with this pompom heart wreath. This colorful wreath will put any guest at ease. You'll want to make one for every room in the house!

To make the pompom heart wreath, you will need:

* Bulky weight yarn in subtle colors

* Metal heart wreath form (found in any craft store)

* Large pompom maker

* Scissors

1 Start by creating about 10 large pompoms. Bulky weight yarn works best for this project.

Tip: Although you could easily adjust the colors, there is something about the subtlety of a subdued color combination that really makes the wreath work.

Wrap the yarn around one side of the pompom maker until there is a large bulge and you can't see the plastic. Repeat this on the other side.

Cut both sides of the yarn while the pompom is still on the maker and trim if necessary. Tie a knot in the middle before releasing the pompom from the maker and trim if necessary.

Tip: When you tie the pompom, be sure to leave the ends long so that you can tie them in step 3.

2 Once the pompoms are made, lay them out in the pattern you envision—leaving the two long yarn ties from each pompom loose.

Gently lay the heart wreath form reverse side up onto the pompom heart you've created.

3 Adjust the placement of the pompoms as needed to fill out the wreath, then start tying the pompoms into place. Use the 3 different metal layers of the wreath form for added stability, tying each pompom through a number of times to hold it firmly in place.

4 Here is your finished pompom wreath! Trim the pompom ties as necessary.

5 Tie a length of the yarn on the back to hang the pompom wreath on a wall or door!